What The Fire Left

Fragments of Faith: A Poet's Search for Meaning

Erica R.C. Kline

BookLeaf Publishing

India | USA | UK

Made with ❤ on the BookLeaf Publishing Platform

www.bookleafpub.in

www.bookleafpub.com

Dedication

First and foremost, to God-
My Restorer, My Teacher, and my Purpose-Giver. Thank
you for granting me the wisdom, reflection, and courage
to share my thoughts, experiences, and heart with
others.
May every word carry the weight of Your grace and
goodness so that those who read may feel Your love as
deeply as I have.

To my family-
The tribe You chose for me.
Thank you for being my greatest earthly blessing.
All of you still here and those of you resting-
I love you- always and forever.

To my friends-
Thank you for standing with me through thick and thin
and for loving me exactly as I am. Your friendship is a
gift I deeply cherish.

To every reader-
I pray these poems bring you comfort, peace, and
stillness. May you find in them a blessing-
a whisper of God's grace meant just for you.

This journey-
From pen to paper-
Has been for one purpose alone:
To bless God,
Not for gain,
But for His glory.

Lord-
Thank You for raising me up,
For restoring my soul,
And for helping me make this dream come true.

All glory to You-
Now and forever.
Amen.

Preface

I always dreamed of writing a book-
I just didn't know *this* would be the book.
Poetry wasn't my plan-
It was just where I *landed*-
Or more truthfully-
Where God *placed* me.

Every poem in these pages were born from brokenness and grace, questions and answers, ashes and Amen. They are not just words on a page- they are wounds that healed, tears that testified, and prayers that turned to praise.

This collection is divided into **three movements**- **Conviction, Encounte**r, and **Discovery**.- because that is how I've come to know God:

First through *Conviction*- when the hollow places of my life were exposed.

Then, through *Encounter*- when grace met me in my emptiness.

And finally, *Discovery*- when I learned that joy truly

does come in the morning.

Each poem is a **vignette**- a snapshot of the soul-
capturing what it means to *wrestle,* to *question,* to
surrender, and to *believe.* You may find yourself in these
pages- *in the breaking, the burning,* or *the blessing.* And
I hope you do.

But above all-
I pray that you find **God** here. The one who restores the
hollow places,
The One who makes ashes holy,
The One who walks with you through the fire-
And leaves you with something beautiful.

This book was never about me-
It was always for Him.
From pen to paper, from ashes to Amen-
This is my offering.
This-
Is what the fire left.

Acknowledgements

No dream is built alone-
and no fire is endured without the hands of others to lift,
love, and guide you through.

First- **TO MY GOD:**
You are the Author and the Finisher.
Thank you refining me, and placing these words in my
heart.
Every poem, every page-
is for Your glory alone.

To my **family** and **Friends:**
Thank you for seeing the talent God has gifted me with
and encouraging me over the years to pursue the arts.
This book carries echoes of your support.
I love you with all of my heart.

To those who inspired, encouraged, and sharpened me
along this journey-
from conversations to prayers to quiet moments of
wisdom- thank you for pouring into me.

Finally-
To the **dreamer in me-**

The one who always wanted to write a book:
You did it.

With a heart full of gratitude-
Erica R.C. Kline

1. The Thorn and the Echo

I have thirsted for more,
yet I have drunk from shallow wells-
mistaking emptiness as virtue,
calling absence a kind of peace.

I ask for purpose,
but the echo returns my own voice-
familiar, insistent,
wearing the mask of revelation.

Confusion isn't new to me.
I've traced its contours in the dark,
felt its weight in rooms
where wrong feels like home
and right, an ill-fitted garment.

By pride comes only strife.
-Proverbs 13:10

Yet pride whispers in my doubts,

in the polished edge of reasoning,
where I mistake intellect for wisdom.

There is more.
I taste it in the silence,
between questions-
sense it in the hollow space
where certainty should dwell.

How unsettling-this tightrope of
belief,
where faith feels less like
homecoming,
and more like exile without end.

Could conviction itself be the
gatekeeper,
holding me back from grace
until I admit
I cannot cross alone?

Lord, teach me silence
not as absence, but as presence.
Still my tongue-
not out of fear, but reverence.

I want to be more

than the sum of my failings,
yet my heart leans into familiar sin
like an old friend.

I have washed feet with unclean
hands,
believing service could mask the
stain.

And still-this thorn remains,
offering no bloom,
yet pulsing with grace
I cannot name.

For it was not the rose,
but the thorn,
that tore the temple veil
and revealed the Christ within.

2. The Shape of Waiting

Is waiting a test of trust,
or an unveiling- slow, sure?
I ask the wind as it brushes past,
pulling the edges of another
stretched hour.

Seconds press down, thick as clay,
molded by impatient hands.
I stand still,
but my thoughts drift-
always drift-
toward what hasn't yet arrived.

Is delay a lock,
or the turning of the key?
Does the spirit wither
under paused skies,
or does it gather,
quiet as moss over stone?

I've stood at thresholds
where promises felt thin as breath,
where the floor beneath me
threatened to disappear.
But even as the minutes dragged,
I felt my spine stacking taller-
a quiet architecture of resolve.

I have learned, in the long pause,
that time is not the enemy.
It's a mirror,
reflecting back the edges of who I
am
when nothing moves
but my own will.

Waiting isn't empty space.
It's a scaffold,
holding the shape
of what's to come.
Not brittle,
but bending with purpose.

So, is waiting a test of trust
or an unveiling- slow, sure?
Maybe the standstill is the shaping,

and the burden we carry
is the bridge we build.

3. This House

Build your house on how you feel-
Call it strong, call it steel.
Stack your walls with pride and will,
paint them bright, and hold them
still.

But feelings shift like winds that
roam.
They stir the dust. They shake the
stone.
Your heart may sing, your heart may
break-
but the heart, my dear, can make
mistakes.

You trust your heart? The heart runs
wild.
It's bold at dawn, but meek by night.
It leads you wrong, it leads you right

but it won't hold when the ground
ignites.

Now, truth-
truth is not a fleeting guest.
It does not bow, it does not rest.
It does not ask how you may feel;
truth stands firm, and truth is real.

You lean on strength? It too will fail-
slipping like rain, snapping like hail.
But faith, when rooted deep in
ground
that does not move, will not fall
down.

And when the winds rise up, as they
do,
when the world shakes the ground
beneath you-
still your walls will stand upright,
not by your strength, but by His
might.

4. Beyond the Weary Vale

We hear the wailing of the wind,
yet still, we pass it by.
It sings of toil, it hums of loss,
yet none will heed its cry.

The earth laments in silent grief,
yet few will bow to know
the ache that lingers in the dust
beneath our weary stride.

But see- the dying evening glows
with hints of golden air
A whisper stirs- the boundless
shore
that waits the weary there.

No tempest shakes the silver gates,
no tear shall stain the ground,
for mercy walks in robes of light
where peace and joy abound.

And there- beyond the pulling stars,
where time and sorrow cease,
a voice shall call the wandering
home
to rest in peace untold.

5. Love Has Not Left the Room

It's easy to examine another's life
while hiding from your own.
Why do we know what's good for
others
but remain lost ourselves?

In her darkest hour,
a mother forgets her own light,
watching shadows take shape
inside her child's mind-
monsters without names,
demons she cannot fight.

The walls of the room hold secrets,
the closet and the bed frame
whisper.
What she once taught now feels
hollow,
truths unraveling in silent spaces.

How does a bond unravel,
thread by thread, between mother
and child?

Her heart, heavy with questions,
seeks refuge in the intangible-
faith, hope, meaning,
from places unknown.

Is love enough when it meets the
edges of the mind?
Can she find herself again,
standing at the threshold,
between love and the unknown?

She listens-
not for answers,
but for the quiet truth beneath the
chaos.

She is here.
He is here.
And love, though fragile,
has not left the room.

6. Sunday Faith, Saturday Face

At eight, you arrived—flowers in one
hand, tequila in the other.

Am I confused?
I don't mean to sound rude,
but I'm a little unglued
since we met in that small Christian group.

You said, "Let's meet—talk faith,
get real about our Christian views."
But somewhere between dinner
and the second glass of booze,
you shifted the conversation—
from Scripture to suggestion,
from faith to fornication.

So I've got a question:
When you drove me home,
with expectation in your eyes,

did you ever stop to wonder
if your heart was telling lies?

Because here's what I know—
if you ever looked inward,
you'd see your pride too.

Why do we fall in love with lies,
dress up deceit with cream cheese,
and call it a pie?

I don't mind asking forward questions,
even if the answers come back
backward—
because I have a sober mind.

Can I pray with you?
My apologies—
will you be offended if I mention
my journey requires modesty?

See, I'm not here to play pretend,
or water down truth just to blend in.
I'm looking for love that mirrors grace—
not just Sunday faith
with a Saturday face.

Thanks for the flowers—
I'll leave the tequila behind.
I've got a different road to follow,
and peace is what I'll find.

7. From the Fall to the Cross

Adam and Eve,
Tempted by forbidden fruit,
though God counseled them with truth.
Humankind-will we ever learn?

The fall of man is sin,
and still-we reach.
For what is just beyond our grasp,
for what will never fill us.

Why do we chase what breaks us?
Why do we hunger for the hollow?
Is it pride that blinds our eyes,
or the illusion that we can follow
our own way, without the weight of
grace?

The serpent's voice still whispers-
not just in the garden,
but in the quiet corners of our hearts-

telling us we can be gods,
that we control our own destinies,
that truth is flexible,
that freedom means no boundaries.

But freedom without truth is a chain,
a promise wrapped in poison.

We crave what is forbidden
because the heart, untethered from God,
seeks to fill a void.
We believe we are missing something-
when in truth,
we already had everything.

We trade Eden for fleeting moments,
wisdom for pride,
covering ourselves with fig leaves of falsehood,
hiding from the One who sees all.

Yet His voice still calls in the garden:
"Where are you?"

And though we run,
though we fall,
grace waits at the gates of Eden,
stretching further

than the curse can reach.

For even in our darkest hour,
the light was never lost.

A tree bore forbidden fruit,
but another tree bore the cross.

And through that sacrifice, we rise,
no longer bound by sin's disguise.

Adam fell,
But Christ arose-
making broken things whole.

And though we stumble,
we are found.
Though we wander,
we are home.

8. A Broken Moment
Turned Holy

I cracked open-
but light poured through the
fractures.
I wept-
not only for the breaking,
but for the self I had clung to,
small, trembling,
afraid to let go.

The questions pierced, sharp as spears:
Why this sorrow? Why this silence?
Had I wandered beyond finding?

But heaven does not speak in thunder alone-
sometimes, it whispers in the wound.

I was not abandoned;
I was being undone-
peeled back to the marrow of my

need,
to the place where flesh fails and
spirit begins.

There, in the wilderness of my undoing,
I found the hands that had never let go.
Not cruel.
Not distant.
But steady.
Sure.
Mending the torn places with gold.

And when I could stand,
I was no longer the same-
Not unbroken,
but made wholly remade.

9. In the Hush, He Spoke

The wind carried more than air today-
a brush of eternity against my skin.

When the weight fell-
doubt, fear, the ache of waiting-
I saw my shadow walking beside me,
no longer alone.

In the hush between heartbeats,
I found You waiting, God-
not distant,
not unseen,
but steady as the tide-
as if You had been there always.

No need to reach,
nor run,
nor grasp-
only to breathe.
Only to see.

And in that seeing,
I was known.
A whisper of Your truth in the stillness,
a promise stitched into the fabric of
time.

With each pulse of creation,
I felt the ground shift-
Your light poured in, dancing,
illuminating paths I once feared to
tread.

Together we stood-
a tapestry of shadow and shine,
threads of mercy binding
the fragile remnants of yesterday
into a dawn made radiant by Your
presence.

10. Where the Willows Sway

I wandered where the willows
swayed,
where golden light through
branches played.
The river hummed a soft refrain,
a voice that knew me- called my
name.

The breeze spun light against my
skin,
a whispered hush, a breath within.
No thunder rolled, no fire burned,
yet in the stillness, truth returned.

The ripples curled, the echoes ran,
as if they'd traced the path I'd
planned.
Yet every stone, each winding bend,
revealed a love that has no end.

I knelt where roots embraced the
stream,
as earth and heaven wove a
dream.
No fear remained, no doubt could
stay-
His presence met me in the sway.

11. Unshaken

At times, I feel heavy,
held down by the weight of earth.
Yet even then, I hear His voice-
like a Father, like a friend,
who called my name before my birth.

His Love lifts me when I fall,
His hands reach out, my chains undone.
A pull that never wavers,
a grace as endless as the sun.

I seek no praise from fleeting men,
nor marvel at their hollow ways.
For in His truth, I stand unshaken,
a child of grace that never fades.

12. A Holy Thirst

Like living water, cleanse my soul
Quench my thirst, restore, make whole.

Flood my heart with mercy deep,
Sanctify me- my soul to keep.

Empower me to boldy stand,
To speak Your truth, to lift Your name.
Let courage rise where fear once lived,
Let fire fall, let faith remain.

Holy Spirit, dwell in me,
Cleanse, renew, and set me free.
Overflow like rivers wide,
Stay within, my soul's abide.

13. Refined in the Flame

I feared the flame,
Its burning edge,
The way it licked at all I'd claimed,
Unraveling my grip on shame.

But You, O Lord,
Are not the storm,
Nor the blaze that strikes to kill—
You are the fire that refines,
Melting doubt, reshaping will.

The embers glow,
My pride undone,
What once was mine,
Now Yours alone.
No ashes left, no chains remain—
Only gold within the flame.

And in the heat, I find my rest,
No longer fighting, no longer stressed.

For in Your hands, my soul is free—
Refined, renewed, made whole in Thee.

14. The Power Was Never in the Pen

From a withered hand and a dried
pen,
no ink to stain the paper.

I press the tip to the page. Nothing.
The words that once flowed like streams
are now dust in my throat, brittle and
unsaid.
Has the well run dry? Has my voice
been spent?

Then- a whisper.
Not from the pen,
Not from my mind,
but from somewhere deeper.

Write.

I hesitate.

What can be written without ink?
What can be spoken when the
tongue is weary?

Yet my hand moves,
tracing unseen lines upon the page.
And before my eyes,
the words appear-
not in ink, but in fire, in light,
in something eternal.

It was never the pen that held the power.

15. Suffering Feels Purple

A sinless man,
a royal King,
gave His life-
for us, for love, for loyalty.

Can you imagine the purpose?
The weight, the obedience?
A lawful man
among lawless men,
carrying out the will of Heaven.

Only the Son could.

The Son,
The Son-
Lift your eyes to the Son.

The clouds shift,
they bow in tandem.
The earth trembles,

she groans,
she weeps,
she feeds.

And the crown-
not gold, but thorns,
pressed deep into the brow of grace.
Blood and mercy drip like wine,
bruises bloom, deep and violet,
spreading like dusk across His skin,
spilling into the soil
as the sky turns it's face away.

Suffering feels purple.

It is the hush before the storm,
the weight of a robe too heavy,
dragging through dust,
bearing the weight of a borrowed cross.

It is the shrouded bruise beneath an
eye,
the tender flesh torn beneath the
lash,
the royal hue of pain that lingers
long after the world forgets.

**Suffering is purple-
the color of Kings,
the shade of surrender,
the stain that will not fade.**

And still, they did not see.
Not in the thorns.
Not in the wounds.
Not in the hands stretched wide
to embrace a world too blind to bow.

16. A Echo of Absence

What do you call a mirror without
glass?
Is it like-
A mind without thoughts,
A heart without feelings,
A soul without spirit?

A man without God
Is simply a godless man-
But God without a man
is still God.

An ocean without life
Still holds water.
A child without guidance
Still longs for a father.

Yet-
Does a flame without warmth stop
burning?

Does a road without travelers forget
its way?
Does the sky without stars shrink in
it's vastness?
Or a seed, buried deep, forget how to bloom?

And if absence teaches-
That a vessel, though hollow,
Still carries the echo of what it was
made for,
That even the void itself can be a canvass
for the infinite-

Then tell me-
Is it the emptiness we fear,
Or the chance it could still be filled?

For what is life without meaning,
If not a question unanswered-
And a heart brave enough-
To keep asking?

17. The Wildness of Grace

Not being in control of your emotions
Is like thinking you can have a sip of
alcohol
After ten years of sobriety.

You can tell yourself-just one taste,
But the rush remembers you-
It knows every door you swore shut.

And suddenly-
You are drowning in the ache
Time never really buried.

Because here's the thing-
Control was never the cure.
Numbness never meant healing.

What if breaking
Is just the beginning?
What if unraveling

Is where truth slips through?

What if holiness
Was never in the holding back-
But in the breaking open?

Because the Spirit moves
Where walls collapse
And hearts are raw enough
To be rewritten.

So let go-
Not to fall,
But to be found
In the wildness
Of grace.

18. Not a Conqueror, but an offering

I was not prepared
For the truth to tear me open,
To strip away the layers
Only God could peel.

The burden was heavy,
The chain was tight-
Dare I name the shame?

Like the woman at the well,
Jesus revealed my past
And offered me living water-
Despite the altars
I built to my ruin.

I asked, "How long have you been waiting for me?"
And my heart heard Him say:
"Since before you knew my name.
Child, let me forgive your past,

Let me heal your pain.
I am the Great I Am,
Your Savior, Your King."

How could I not listen closely?
How did I not hear sooner?
My path to salvation-
Was like Saul's road to Damascus.

He changed me from the inside out,
Breathed new breath into me-
Cleansed my dirty hands-
Gave me life instead of death.

He took the scars-
And made them a story.
Took the chains-
And made them a testimony,
Took my suffering-
And made it holy.

So here I am-
Not a conqueror-
But an offering.

I will not turn back-
Even if it costs me all.

19. In His Time

I wanted the promise
But not the patience.
I prayed for open doors
And grew restless in the hallway.

I thought waiting
Would feel like peace,
But it felt like silence-
Like knocking
On a door
That won't open yet.

I have cried-
"How long, Lord?"
But Heaven's answer
Has been the same-
"Trust me."

Abraham waited-
While the stars kept their promise,

Even when his arms stayed empty.
Joseph dreamed-
While prison walls whispered
That dreams deceive.
Hannah wept-
Before her womb knew joy.
And Lazarus-
Lay in death
Until You called him forth.

So who am I
To demand a clock
From the Author of eternity?

If You are still writing-
Then I will keep waiting.
If You are still weaving-
Then I will trust every thread-
Even the tangled ones.

For I know-
When the answer comes-
It will be the full one.
And when that time arrives,
It will be holy.

So I will stand-

Not in certainty,
But in trust.
Not in impatience,
But in hope.
Not with clenched fists,
But with open hands-
Ready to receive-
In Your time.

20. Joy is Coming

To the weary-
To the poor-
To the widowed-
To the desolate and the afraid-
To the persecuted,
The homeless,
The starving-
This is for you.

I know-
The nights are long
When hunger is your companion,
When the world forgets
You have a name,
When hope feels like a rumor
You stopped believing in.

I know what it is-
To weep without words,
To pray without answers,

To search the sky
And only see the weight of night.

But listen-
The silence is not the end.
The darkness is not your forever.

The ground you called barren
Will bloom again.
The tears you thought were wasted
Will water a new beginning.

Because there is a God
Who sees the unseen,
Who counts every unheard cry,
Who bends low
To lift the broken.

He does not crush
The weary reed.
He does not snuff out
The flickering flame.

And when He restores,
It is not half-
It is whole.

So-
how do you keep going
When the road is long?
Rest, but don't stop.
When the night is cold-
Hold on to every sliver of light.
When your heart is heavy-
Let the tears fall,
But don't let them harden you.

When you feel forgotten-
Remember:
The One who made you
Has never lost you.

And if you cannot run-
Crawl.
If you cannot sing-
Whisper.
If you cannot believe-
Borrow the faith of another.

But-
Do not stop.
Do not stop.
Do not-
Stop.

Because joy is coming.
It always comes.
And when it does,
It will not come quietly.

It will break through the cracks
Of everything you thought was dead.
It will burst from the ruins
And flood the ground you mourned.

And when it comes,
You will not be who you were-
You will be
Who you survived to become.

The ashes
Will be crowned with beauty.
The scars
Will sing your story.
The sorrow
Will become your song.

So-
to the weary-
To the poor-
To the forgotten and the afraid-

Keep going.
Keep breathing.
Keep hoping.
Keep praying.

Because joy is coming-
And when it comes-
The world that broke you
Will not recognize you.

21. Your Amen

You have walked through fire-
But you are not consumed.
You have tasted sorrow-
But joy has found you.

You have fought through darkness-
But you are made of light.
The battle did not break you-
It built you.
The fire did not finish you-
It forged you.

Do not measure your life
By the wounds that tried to claim you,
But by the grace that carried you through.

Do not count what darkness stole-
Count what light restored.

You are not the victor-

But stand in His victory.
You are not the healer-
But you bear the marks of His
healing.

The battle was His-
The triumph is yours-
Because the cross-
Was enough.

So- how do you live now?
You live-
As one who has seen the night
And believes the morning.
You Live-
As one who knows the weight of
sorrow-
But chooses the song of praise.
You live-
Not as who you were,
But as who you are becoming.

And when you go-
Go with your heart-
Open wide.
Go with your hand-
Ready to bless-

Go with your voice-
Unashamed to testify:

That you have seen the valley-
And walked through it.
You have counted the cost-
And chosen the cross.
That you have met the Truth-
And lived it.

So-
This is not the end.
This is your beginning.
This is not the closing-
This is the calling.

And this-
Is your Amen.

So be it.
So live it.
So carry it-
To the ends of the earth.